A
GUIDE
for
Writing Teachers

How to Build Effective
Writing Communities
in College

Dr. LaRonce M. Hendricks

authorHOUSE®

AuthorHouse™
1663 Liberty Drive
Bloomington, IN 47403
www.authorhouse.com
Phone: 1 (800) 839-8640

Published by AuthorHouse 06/22/2017

ISBN: 978-1-5246-9739-6 (sc)
ISBN: 978-1-5246-9738-9 (e)

Library of Congress Control Number: 2017909884

Print information available on the last page.

CONTENTS

ABSTRACT

This guide: "How to Build Effective Writing Communities in College" put forth helpful tips to aid any teacher to motivate students toward self-directness to stir a spirit of inquiry. It is a helping aid for building students with low confidence in writing to write with high confidence levels. The guide's theoretical view builds upon the following: constructivist perspectives, andragogy, and educational psychology. It provides thirteen tips for creating a positive classroom environment for writing.

ACKNOWLEDGEMENTS

I am most thankful to Dr. Charles Backes, who provided the guidance at Valdosta State University to spark my interest in writing a guide to aid college composition teachers. Also, my thanks go to Dr. Katheleen Fabrikant, who helped me to begin this journey; she said, "You can do it," and I believed! You encouraged me to persevere, and you supported me on this journey until the end. I am also thankful to Dr. Jerry Siegrist, who kept me focused and on track; and to Dr. Iris Ellis, who inspired me: "You have a gift to write," I humbly received her words of affirmation to write this manuscript.

DEDICATION

I would like to dedicate this book to my grandchildren Taylor, Cameron, Miya, Makaila, Kennedy, Madison, Maurice, Leonard, and Caleb. This book lays the pathway for you all. As your grandmother, I have demonstrated that you can do all things through Christ Jesus. Now I pass this writing mantle on you all to fulfill your educational journey. Most of all, I ask that each of you take education to another dimension— not only to contribute to the wealth of knowledge to educate your generation, but also to wipe illiteracy out of the family lineage. May God strengthen you all until the end of time.

CHAPTER 1

Introduction

The National Assessment of Adult Literacy (2012) reported that 87% of Americans lack the skills to write. According to Chantrill (2008), most college students cannot write a decent paper. From a recent study, some first-year college college students found difficulty writing in college. For that, many have either failed college writing, or dropped out of academic programs altogether because they dread college writing. Levine and Kirst (2015) alluded that More students are enrolling in college, but they are not prepared for the rigors of college writing.

According to Levine and Kirst (2015), the 2002 No Child Left Behind law did not enforce grammar instructions, nor did it assess grammar instructions under the common core standards. The act relied heavily upon the grammar instructions learned in grade school; however, they claimed that "not all those diagramming sentences we did as children stuck" (p. 16); in other words, what little grammar education was imparted did not make much of a difference.

Gabriel (2014) added that most students are taking up to six years to graduate from college because students are lacking in basic writing skills. In addition, the non-profit Complete College America (CCAE, 2014) reported that students at a two-year college spent approximately $15,933 for every extra additional year, beyond the requisite two years, on tuition fees and room and board (CCAE, 2014).

A key problem is that negative predispositions toward writing among college students could affect a student's ability to communicate using written methods in composition courses in academic programs (Lindemann & Anderson, 2001). Lindemann and Anderson (2001) indicated that certain negative predispositions could cause mental constraints for some students.

Moreover, some students had an unreasonable fear of writing that came from the belief that writing represented failure or bad grades. The notion that "teachers have always found fault with my writing" (p. 15) can set up a negative thought cycle.

Finally, without placing the blame on who, why, or how, educators must deliver the knowledge students will need to develop and improve their competency skills to write and express themselves clearly and concisely at college. Speedy mastery of competency skills will help close achievement gaps, reduce time spent in college, and increase retention rates (CCR, 2014; Dobrin, 2015).

With the immersion of technology" (CRLA, 2015, Southeast Symposium, p. 1), institutions across the globe are faced with daily challenges to graduate students on time.

The Purpose

The purposes of this new publication are threefold: 1) it was produced for busy writing instructors who may not have the time to read a lengthy and complex text book. Instead, the guide is for instructors who have less than one hour to spare. It is formatted as an easy read. The guide put forth 13 helpful tips useful for lessening the effects of negative predispositions. 2) The guide suggests alternative approaches for building an effective classroom environment to motivate fearful writers to enjoy a meaningful experience writing college papers, and 3) it represents the voices of those struggling writers who want writing instructors to understand how negative predispositions can affect one's ability to write.

Definition of Terms

Andragogy: "the art and science of adult learning" (Knowles, 1989, p. 69).

Constructivism: "a learning theory about the nature of

knowing, internal aspects of learning" (Ormond, 2009, p. 18).

Georgia's State Board of Education mandatory competencies: "Abilities and qualities necessary for students to reach their potential as individuals and citizens" (Paterson, 2008, p. 23 [G.A.R. 160-4-2-. 01 (2) (c)).]

Learning: "a long-term change in mental representations or associations due to experience" (Ormond, 2009, p. 18).

Writing: "a process of communication that uses a conventional graphic system to convey a message to a reader" (Lindemann & Anderson, 2001, p. 10).

Predisposition: "a tendency to hold a particular attitude, or act in a particular way" (English Oxford Living Dictionaries, 2016).

Negative predispositions: to feel a premonition, apprehension, or fear that something bad or unpleasant will happen in the course (Hendricks, 2017, p. 11).

Core Competencies

Before a student can receive credit for three-semester hours, the student must successfully show mastery skills in all five domains based on the Georgia State Board of Education core competencies. Paterson (2008) explained the importance of the Georgia State Board of Education core competencies for an English 1010 course. Most technical colleges would follow version (201003L) core competencies protocol. Students who enroll in non-degree programs, regardless of the course offerings selected, must take an English 1010 course. Most English 1010 instructors are required to implement appropriate lessons to aid students in writing efficiently, so they can write as productive citizens. A typical semester lesson plan would entail the production of the following: essays, business letters, and a research paper (TCSG, 2015). Each student must receive a mastery grade of 'C' or better before he or she can receive credit.

CHAPTER 2

Psychological Barriers

Lindemann and Anderson (2001) surmised that negative predispositions were mental constraints. That mental constraints were psychological barriers derived from years of red ink marks put on students' graded writing assignments by writing teachers. That "Red ink marks symbolize either the color of defeat or the color of authority for some students" (p. 15). Therefore, some students will come to the learning environment with an unreasonable amount of fear that stems from the belief that writing represents failure or bad grades. The idea that "teachers have always found fault with my writing" (p. 15).

Furthermore, Ormond (2009) alluded that psychological barriers were embedded in the human memory and that negative predispositions were associated with bad grades from the red ink marks. That the human brain has the capacity to save negative information to the memory bank. For example, a student thinking and rethinking about bad grades, or thinking about failing the course, or believing that "Oh, I don't know grammar" (Elbow, 1998, p. 168) gets inscribed in the human memory. Then the human brain creates pattern associations that lies dormant in the human memory for years until a student begins to write a complex writing assignment. Then negative predipositions can resurface in the memory and block a student's ability to make contact on paper.

What is Making Contact on Paper?

Making contact on paper is a term used by Lindemann and Anderson (2001). As defined by Lindemann and Anderson, making contact on paper is a student's ability to express in writing his or her experiences, beliefs, or "complicated configurations of knowledge" (p. 15).

Thus, Lindemann and Anderson (2001) concurred that over time, students affected with negative predispositions would begin associating complex writing assignments such as essays or research papers with bad grades.

Finally, Lindemann and Anderson (2001) closed the discussion by saying that students affected by psychological barriers had difficulty with the concept of failing the course, so they would either drop the course before the end of term or would quit school altogether and walk away in defeat (Lindemann & Anderson, 2001)

What is Negative Predispositions?

Negative predisposition is defined as a "Student's premonitions, anxiety, or fear that something bad or unpleasant will happen in the course" (Hendricks, 2017, p. 11).

Below are ten identifiable negative predispositions:

1. Overthinking about getting bad grades
2. Writing unfamiliar topics
3. Lacking vocabulary skills
4. Lacking comprehensive skills
5. Lacking basic skills to write at a college level
6. Demeaning responses from writing teachers
7. Walking away feeling humiliated
8. Seeking help for basic skills to write
9. Perceiving that basic skills are learned in grade school
10. Asking basic grammar questions openly in class is embarrassing

How Negative Predispositions Could Affect Students' Ability to Write in College?

To conceptualize how negative predispositions can affect a student's ability to write in college secondary sources written by educational writing experts such as Dobrin (2015), Lindemann and Anderson (2001), Elbow (1998), and Spivey (2006).

Firstly, Dobrin (2015) asserted that college students wrote in college for the following three reasons: (1) learning: students would share in an experience of learning to write in new and different situations and would write to learn from their writing; (2) participating: students would write reflective papers about their experiences and their role in decision-making; and (3) expressing: students would write to express their ideas in writing.

Secondly, Dobrin (2015), Lindemann and Anderson (2001), and Elbow (1998) agreed that college students would learn to write most effectively by using a conventional graphic system to convey a message to the reader. This conventional graphic system most typically consists of a seven-step process: (1) pre-writing, (2) rough draft, (3) peer editing, (4) revising, (5) editing, (6) final draft, and (7) publishing.

Thirdly, Spivey (2006) held that when students engage in the pre-writing process, they must brainstorm to generate ideas for writing. In the initial pre-writing process, most students would chart, create story webs, develop graphic organizers, or develop a word list from which to work, depending on their preferred learning methods; then they would decide upon the type of writing and determine the purpose and the audience for their piece (Spivey, 2006).

In addition, Lindemann and Anderson (2001) and McLaughlin (2010) promoted the idea of implementing a pre-writing diagnostic. McLaughlin (2010) believed that students affected by negative predispositions could be identified in the initial pre-writing phase. For the most part, students affected by negative predispositions have difficulties relating old information to new information to express ideas in writing. Specifically, students affected by mental constraints would find that spontaneous writing assignments represented a less comfortable expressive medium than the human voice.

Lindemann and Anderson (2001) wrote that students affected by negative predispositions had difficulty recalling basic grammar, such as the core subject, prepositions and prepositional phrases, word order, words that cannot be verbs, verb forms and tense, and so on; these issues were due to the anxiety produced by their mental constraints and the possibility of not being able to make contact on paper.

How to Identify Students with Negative Predispositions?

College writing teachers can lessen the negative effects of students' negative predispositions toward writing, but instructors must first identify the affected students (Chantrill, 2008).

Lindemann and Anderson (2001) and McLaughlin (2010) advised on how to identify students with negative predispositions. They suggested giving students a pre-writing diagnosis.

McLaughlin (2010) added that students affected with negative predispositions would find spontaneous writing assignments uncomfortable; thus, when writing teachers announce graded writing assignments on the spot, or announce an assignment on unfamiliar topics, students affected with negative predispositions will become apprehensive, or reluctant, fearful, and will not make contact on paper.

Chantrill (2008), Dobrin (2015), Haley and Alsweel (2012), and Ormond (2009), added if a student has difficulty critically thinking through complex readings, and if a student is lacking skills to problem solve; this too would cause complications and can hinder a student's ability to write because he or she cannot synthesize the information.

Critical Thinking and the Writing Process

Scriven and Paul (1996) believed that "critical thinking [is] the intellectually disciplined process of actively and skillfully conceptualizing, applying, analyzing, synthesizing, and or evaluating information gathered from, or generated by, observation, experience, reflection, reasoning, or communication, as a guide to belief and action" (pp. 151–156). This process can be taught through writing, but students must engage with the process.

Most writing teachers on college campuses will implement lessons designed to achieve the following standard learning objectives: communication, critical thinking, and problem solving:

> Communication: Students will demonstrate communication using language appropriate for diverse audiences and purposes, including the ability to speak, write, and otherwise express oneself clearly and cogently.

> Critical thinking: Students will demonstrate the ability to examine, analyze, and compare alternatives to identify and challenge assumptions; develop alternative solutions and/or strategies while applying practical and

ethical implications; and construct sound arguments and evaluate the arguments of others.

Problem solving: Students will demonstrate locating relevant information and sources, judging the reliability of those sources, and evaluating the evidence contained in those sources as they construct arguments, make decisions, and solve problems. (TCSG, 2016, p. 1)

However, many of the writing experts agree that some students who enter college are not mentally ready to write (Booth, 1963; Chantrill, 2008; Dobrin, 2015; Hayes, 2016; Lindemann & Anderson, 2001). Hayes (2016) wrote, "We are asking [students] to dive into complex [writing] and texts and understand them, so we need to teach them how to [write] and read complex sentences" (p. 1).

In addition, Chantrill (2008), Dobrin (2015), and Haley & Alswell, (2012) concurred that most college students could not identify complex sentences or understand how to synthesize complex texts. Moreover, Lindeman and Anderson cited Booth (1963), who stated, "Every paper a student will write in college will require a slightly different balancing act" (p. 18).

Overall, these authors have promoted the idea that

writing was a cognitive process that had to be acquired and honed.

Summary

In conclusion, writing academic papers can be challenging for some first-year college students. Research has indicated that negative predispositions toward writing can cause mental constraints. Lindemann and Anderson (2001) suggested that negative predispositions form mental barriers, often generated because of years of seeing red ink markings on graded writing assignments. Due to certain cognitive patterns, negative predispositions can become embedded in the human memory and may cause some students anxiety, fear, or negative feelings before complex writing assignments. Students may associate such red ink markings on graded written assignments with defeat or failure. Statistical reports have revealed that a high percentage of American citizens lack the basic skills to write in socially required contexts (NAAL, 2012). With these challenges in mind, the goal of this study was to identify and elucidate the meaning of negative predispositions based on students' perceptions of writing in an English 1010 course and to seek adult learning strategies and classroom management practices to lessen the effects of negative predispositions in college writing or composition courses.

CHAPTER 3

The Learning Process

In 2009, Pennsylvania State University researcher Jeanne Ellis Ormond provided insight into the processes of learning, cognition, and memory, and how each differed in teaching adult learners aged 18 to 24. Ormond espoused that "[the] human memory operates and adds meaning; memory refers to learners' ability to 'save' things [mentally] that they have learned" (p. 24).

Learning, as Ormond (2009) defined it, is "a long-term change in mental representations or associations due to experience" (p. 18). Here, Ormond was implying that a student would not simply learn by absorbing information like a sponge, but that knowledge and understanding would require a "process of making, actively and intentionally constructing, and knowledge" (p. 21). Learning is a natural process and learning processes are dialectical and cyclical (Mackeracher, 2006). This is a vital concept in constructivist theory.

According to Ormond (2009), learning is a cognitive process that involves the ongoing construction and fine tuning of thought, "building on while restructuring prior knowledge, skills, and experiences" (p. 96). If young adult Millennial learners affected by negative predispositions could come to associate new information with either prior knowledge or with their life experiences, they would experience meaningful and effective learning in writing courses. Unfortunately, few class instructors seem to be actively helping them to make these connections (Chantrill. 2008; Dobrin, 2015; TCSG, 2013).

In her work, Ormond's "Figure 2.4: Model of Human Memory" (2009, p. 25) displayed underlying factors involving "in-depth cognitive processes in connecting new information to prior knowledge." Ormond theorized that when young students focused on a particular stimulus, "attention in the memory process can occur" (p. 26). However, the memory process in students affected by negative predispositions is unique. Before a stimulus can trigger a memory, human attention must flow freely, but negative predispositions block those stimulus triggers from flowing freely. This was why students affected by negative predispositions experience a real disconnect, not only with the writing activity at hand, but with their peers and with their teachers (Lindemann & Anderson, 2001).

Moreover, Ormond (2009) described the following three different connections to knowledge:

1. Declarative knowledge: the nature of how things are, were, or will be
2. Procedural knowledge: the knowledge of how to do something (e.g., skill)
3. Conceptual knowledge: a grouping of objects or events that have something in common (p. 26)

Ormond's conceptualization of knowledge can provide composition teachers with insightful information as to why students affected by negative predispositions may stop participating in class and why they slowly fade away from composition courses. These concepts put forth by Ormond can help writing teachers build upon the positive to lessen the effects of negative predispositions. Writing professionals may consider implementing instructional activities that involve life-experiences.

In conclusion, writing teachers know that good writing can be taught, but educators may need to do extraordinary things to teach it well. Applying Ormond's theories on cognitive learning and writing may help bring about the change institutions need to stay competitive in global markets (Levine & Kirst, 2015). The information provides professional writing teachers more insight on Millennials' thinking and learning process. Given the vast potential of these theories, other educators in the fields of education, psychology, political science, and history may want to embrace these concepts as well.

Ormond (2009) believed learning had three constructive parts. First, it created long-term change within a learner; it was not a quick "transitory use of information" (p. 18). Unlike remembering someone's phone number long enough to call it and then forgetting it shortly after, in this concept, true learning was natural and long-term. Secondly, learning involved "mental representations or associations" (p. 18) based on lasting patterns that an individual's brain formed after experiencing a "change due to experience" (p. 18). Thirdly, Ormond stated that learning was not an attribute of works of "physiological maturation" (p. 18) but rather the process of becoming mature through mental development and growth.

Ormond (2009) and Smith and Morris (2014) cited Carl Jung to explain four main personality dichotomies that could affect learning:

1. Extroverted vs. introverted: Extroverted individuals like talking with others and learning through experience, whereas introverts prefer thinking alone about ideas.

2. Sensing vs. intuitive: Sensing types prefer working with concrete details and tend to be patient, practical, and realistic. Intuitive types like abstractions and are creative, impatient, and theory-oriented.

3. Thinking vs. feeling: Thinking types tend to base decisions on objective criteria and logical principles; feeling types are subjective and consider the impact of a decision on other people.
4. Judging vs. perceiving: Judging types are time-oriented and structured, whereas perceivers are spontaneous and flexible. (Ormond, 2009, p. 6)

Knowing how individuals learn and how they process knowledge, as well as understanding cognitive, memory, and learning processes may help educators "unlock" the learning potential of students affected by negative predispositions; however, doing so will require writing teachers to create lessons adapted to individual students' personality traits.

Ormond (2005) assessed students in grade levels 6–8 and 9–12 to determine their personality traits and produced five learning strategies.

Grade Levels 6–8

- Predominance of rehearsal as a learning strategy
- Greater abstractness and flexibility in categories used to organize information
- Emergence of elaboration as an intentional learning strategy

Grade Levels 9–12

- Continuing reliance on rehearsal as an intentional learning strategy, especially by low-achieving students
- Increasing use of elaboration and organization to learn, especially by high achieving students (Ormond, 2005, p. 35)

In short, individual students' cognitive and memory abilities were different, particularly at different ages.

Lastly, Smith and Morris (2014) conceptualized the *schemata* learning strategy.

Smith and Morris (2014) held that schemata learning is a product of our imagination that "schemata are the [driving] force of active learning" (p. 271). Schemata was not driven by rehearsal or memorization (Smith & Morris, 2014). Drawing upon this concept, the idea that schemata learning may move students with negative predispositions toward active learning because students can form images before charting, creating story webs, developing graphic organizers.

CHAPTER 4

Basic Underlying Assumptions of Educational Psychology

Learning, Cognition, Memory, and Developmental Trends

Basic underlying assumptions of educational psychology have typically focused on key aspects of psychology: thinking, learning, development, motivation, and assessment of human characteristics. Ormond (2009) found in, a study by Piaget, that young adult Millennial students could learn new information based on prior knowledge, but these students were still developing mentally and they lacked the experience to make good decisions concerning their own education. Students' mental development involved a continual process of refining, building on, and occasionally reconfiguring previous experiences. Ormond therefore concluded that young adult Millennials needed help to make decisions in the classroom.

Developmental Trends

Ormond (2009) believed that most Baby Boomers and Gen Xers would come to the adult learning environment with a greater volume of experiences and more physiological maturity than young adult Millennials. As a result, Baby Boomers and Gen Xers made better decisions about their educational needs. To support this hypothesis, Ormond identified several developmental trends that provided evidence that young adult Millennial students would rely on defenders, instructors, and parents to channel them toward the right decisions during complex writing assignments (Lindemann & Anderson, 2001; Ormond, 2009).

The work of Hershey, Blanchard, and Johnson (1976) supports Ormond's developmental assessment. Hershey et al., claimed that Baby Boomers and Gen Xers had a richer volume of experiences and an eagerness to learn than the Millennial generation. For example, when most Baby Boomers and Gen Xers went to college, they earned a mastery grade of 'C' on the Georgia state's core competency exam. These students developed the skills to write successfully in college and in other situations; therefore, they graduated on time, gained access to more life opportunities, and experienced success in their careers (NCES, 2013).

Reese (2011) concurred that students between ages 18 to 24 relied heavily on the support of their parents because they were not mentally ready to handle a disciplined lifestyle; accordingly, they would not take on adult-like responsibilities. On the other hand, Freire (2005) argued that when students came to the adult learning environment, the teacher would control what they learned; they would not need to take on adult responsibility for their learning. For these students, learning something new came through memorizing information "narrated by the teacher" (p. 80). Nor would students practice any act of cognition or employ critical thinking skills, because students were treated as mere objects that were banking concepts deposited by the instructor (p. 73). Therefore, teachers became the subject of the educational process. This underlying concept noted that writing teachers assumed the responsibility for making decisions about what students learned, how they would learn it, and when it was learned (Freire, 2005).

Summary

In closing, change can come to our institutions, but writing teachers and institutions will need a better understanding of negative predispositions before they can help lessen their negative effects. Writing was identified as a constructivist process because learners create knowledge rather than simply receive it (Ormond, 2009). The cognitive process development consists of a continual process of fine-tuning and adjusting one's mental state based on the use of prior knowledge, skills, and experiences (Ormond, 2009). Brookfield (2006) explained the importance of adopting better classroom practices, which would require writing teachers to take on more work-related responsibilities to ensure student success.

Ormond (2009) held that mental constraints could block the cognitive learning process. Dobrin (2015) stressed that writing procedures would involve similar overlapping processes: (1) pre-writing, (2) rough draft, (3) peer editing, (4) revising, (5) editing, (6) final draft, and (7) publishing. This, according to Dobrin, was since college writing entailed writing within English, science, social studies, health education, and psychology courses. Ormond (2009) wrote that some developmental traits of young adult Millennials would fall in the same category, in many respects, as those of adolescents. This was based on her research into students in grade levels 9–12, which found that age determined developmental trends and cognitive development. Young adult Millennial students affected by negative predispositions do not yet have the necessary life experiences to make good decisions while they draft complex writing assignments and may not have the self-discipline to engage in autonomous learning.

Lastly, students affected by negative predispositions will need some support systems in place before they can internalize information to write complex papers in college.

CHAPTER 5

Thirteen Helpful Tips for Building an Effective Writing Environment in College

The literature was purposefully reviewed for solutions that could help build effective writing communities (Bland, Melton, Wells & Bigham, 2012; Burke, 2002; Brookfield, 2006; Carter, 2007; Chantrill, 2008; Costa & Garmston, 1985; Elbow, 1998; Falk & Blaylock, 2010; Freire & Macedo, 1921; Green, 2000; Holly, 2014; Holt et al., 2013; Howe & Strauss, 2007; Knowles, 1989; Knowles, 1989b; Knowles et al., 2007; Lacefield, 2014; Lindemann & Anderson, 2001; Merriam, Caffarella, & Baumgartner, 2007; McLaughlin, 2010; Napier & Gershenfeld, 2004; Schon, 1987; Surowiecki, 2005; Valez, Cano, Whittington, & Wolf, 2011).

However, Charmaz (2006) believed more emphasis should be on the views, values, beliefs, feelings, assumptions, and ideologies of the individual researcher and that a researcher should advocate his or her own personal values, experiences, and priorities to enhance the writing. Ormond (2009) surmised that a study should depend on a researcher's views about his or her experiences, situations, and relationships as embedded within the research. Therefore, the author relied heavily on respondents' descriptive written responses, collected from a Qualtrics Online Survey, and on the researcher's own views, values, beliefs, experiences, feelings, assumptions, and ideologies, along with concepts promulgated by experts in the field of adult education and educational psychology to put forth vital information for a guide on, "How to Build Effective Writing Communities in College? This information for a guide is twofold: 1) for lessening the negative effects of predispositions, and 2) for building upon the positive to enhance the college writing experience.

An Analysis for Developing a Guide

The first step in developing this guide was to carefully assess the four transcripts; 24 significant statements were extracted with formulated meanings. The second step was to link five themes, which resulted from arranging the formulated clusters. The third step was to write a guide with suitable strategy types for busy writing instructors who may not have the time to read a lengthy and complex book. Instead, the guide is intended for instructors who have less than an hour to spare, formatted as an easily read guide with 13 helpful tips for lessening the effects of negative predispositions toward writing in first-year college composition courses. It will serve as a resource to communicate with writing teachers, representing the voices of young adult Millennial students who desire to be heard.

How to Break the Ice?

The week before a new semester, writing teachers must begin planning ways to make students feel comfortable (Green, 2000; Schon, 1987). This may require thinking out of the box. Writing teachers can consider introducing an icebreaker, playing games, or bringing in food. The goal is to break the tension in the classroom and to get students acquainted. Similar to a flight attendant who smiles, instructs passengers, and kindly explains the airline procedures, writing teachers will want to make students feel comfortable. Then, once the tension is eased, the teacher can begin with an opening presentation (Green, 2000; Schon, 1987). Another way to ease the tension is to decide upon a positive statement, quote, or a philosophy to represent the class—perhaps something like "quitting is not an option" or "failing is not an option"

(Old English proverb). Positive statements can not only help break the ice, but can set the tone for a positive classroom atmosphere.

How to Create a Positive Classroom Atmosphere?

Writing teachers can create a positive classroom environment early in the semester (Green, 2000). Once the teacher has decided upon a positive quote, statement, or philosophy, he or she should inscribe the positive quote, statement, or innovative philosophy on the class syllabus and within the Blackboard Learning online environment, if the college uses one. It becomes a self-fulfilling prophecy for students; instead of thinking about the negative, they can begin thinking about the positive. It also becomes an agreement of sorts between the students and the instructor to support success (Green, 2000). Moreover, it will serve as a continuous reminder that the teacher can't give up on his or her students. Further, it can help lessen negative predispositions. For the second half of the course, writing instructors will explain the positive quote, statement, or innovative philosophy and integrate it within both lessons and the classroom environment (Carter, 2007). In this model, an instructor's goal is to ease students' anxiety and fears within 30 minutes or before the class ends.

How to Shift to an Authoritative Teaching Practice?

Authentic, trusting, and caring. Following the explanation of the positive quote, statement, or innovative philosophy, it is important that students see writing teachers as authentic, trusting, and caring. All of us have a human side. Therefore, it is important for students to see that we as educators are *authentic, trusting,* and *caring* (Brookfield, 2006). Doing so will require writing teachers to shift to an authoritative teaching practice and abandon authoritarianism. In an authoritative teaching practice, instructors are authentic, trusting, and caring; whereas, an "authoritarian teaching practice instructors will impose their force by using institutional power (Freire & Macedo, 1921).

Freire and Macedo (1921) revealed that authoritative teachers can earn students' respect and keep them engaged longer. Moreover, the *authoritative teaching practice* has been highly praised by adult education experts, according to Holt et al. (2013). To shift to an authoritative practice, writing instructors must be as transparent as possible. Letting students know about your humble beginnings can bring about a connection with your students. Students want to hear about why you decided to major in your specific field of study. A teacher's story is important to students. It gives students a glimpse of their own future.

For instance, I had an instructor who shared her humble beginnings as an adult educator. As a master's-level student, it gave me a glimpse into my future as an adult educator. Lindemann and Anderson (2001) and Chantrill (2008) believed students need to mentally see themselves passing the course, and they need to continuously hear positive affirmation.

How to Initiate Learning Incentives?

Learning incentives can help build confidence and self-worth in adult learners (Bland, Melton, Wells & Bigham, 2012; Burke, 2002; Carter, 2007; Merriam et al., 2007). Burke (2002) and Merriam, Caffarella, and Baumgartner (2007) explained that learning incentives are internal motivators that adult learners can find fulfilling. Subject-matter activities such as complex reading assignments, homework assignments, and other course work can become incentives to motivate students. In this context, learning incentives may involve bonus points built into the course's grading system to offset other scores (Green, 2000); these points can be earned through completing additional work that helps advance students' skills. To introduce such an incentive system, writing teachers should explain options for additional points while introducing the course's syllabus.

Most importantly, writing teachers should clearly explain that learning incentives are for students who are willing to take responsibility for their own learning. The learning incentives are in place for those students who have problems in one area but who are willing to do additional work to gain skills to improve their learning outcomes (Green, 2000). This will boost students' morale; merely knowing that learning incentives are built into the course's grading system may ease their minds about failing. For that reason, writing teachers should wait to introduce the full syllabus until after they have explained the learning incentives or bonus points.

How to Introduce the Course's Syllabus?

State institutions typically mandate the course's syllabus. Syllabi serve as templates for executing learning activities mandated by the state core competencies (TCSG, 2015). When introducing the course syllabus, explain the institution's role in mandating it, and explain the role of an instructor (Schon, 1987). With that background, students will not blame the writing instructor for adhering to state-mandated learning objectives. Moreover, this is an opportunity to demonstrate your authority as the expert in the field. Because a positive atmosphere has been created, students will welcome the information. This will set the bar for building an effective writing community and establish the writing instructor's expectations and goals for achieving a mastery grade of 'C' or better. Once the writing instructor has built a platform, express the expectations regarding attendance, class participation, late assignments, test makeups, etc.

How to Lead Students in Classroom Discussions?

Once the syllabus has been introduced, writing teachers should repeat the semester theme, such as "quitting is not an option" or "failing is not an option." This will include expressing a willingness to meet each learner's individual learning needs. Pause for a moment and take a reflective stance, looking around the classroom at students' facial expressions (Brookfield, 2006). Following a three-minute pause, open the floor for discussions, questions, or concerns about the syllabus. Writing teachers can feel confident in doing so because they have set a positive atmosphere. Even millennial students will adhere to the demands outlined because they have seen an authentic, trusting, and caring person willing to help them to succeed (Howe & Strauss, 2007).

How to Attentively Hear Students' Concerns?

As students share their concerns or ask questions about the syllabus, writing instructors should listen attentively (Schon, 1987). As students express their concerns, teachers can either make mental notes or written notes to allow them to properly address individual concerns during the class. If overly concerned students show signs of anxiety or fear, writing teachers may want to consider making a few adaptations to the syllabus where appropriate.

Teachers may consider implementing andragogy-based activities. Andragogy entails a collaborative approach with a shared focus (Dictionary of Human Resources, 2006; Knowles, 1989; Knowles, 1989b; Knowles et al., 2007); in these activities, the teacher and students collaborate to come up with appropriate learning assignments that will bring about fruitful gains.

Finally, if writing teachers have executed the plan properly, two things may happen. Firstly, if the introduction has been properly executed, those students who were in class the first day will take it upon themselves to find their peers who did not attend class; they will be enticed to spread the good news (Falk & Blaylock, 2010). Secondly, students will either build upon the positive atmosphere set by the teacher or try to tear it down. Therefore, writing instructors should continue building upon the positive foundations for students in the course; keep the discussions open and ensure a safe learning environment to stir a spirit of inquiry. Composition teachers will begin noticing their students are more talkative, asking questions and demonstrating a mindset to learn.

How to Create Synergy in the Classroom?

In 2004, Napier and Gershenfeld discussed the term "synergy" in the educational field. They endorsed the concept that people in large gatherings released a tremendous flow of synergy, based on the concept that two or more people are better than one. People stimulate others in group activities to supplement their own weaknesses and abilities although "the amount of the sum is not greater than the whole" (Napier & Gershenfeld, 2004, p. 46). According to Surowiecki (2005), information is most useful when it is not placed in the hands of one person, but distributed across many students.

Researchers have also concluded that teacher commitments and peer support are key elements for building and stimulating effective learning communities. A learning strategy endorsed by Valez, Cano, Whittington, and Wolf (2011) endorsed peer-paired teaching and group work for sparking synergy in classrooms.

How to Implement Peer Pairing and Group Work?

Peer-paired teaching and group work can spark synergy in a classroom (Valez, Cano, Whittington, & Wolf, 2011). Peer-paired teaching and group work are ways to teach complex assignments. According to Valez et al., (2011), peer-paired teaching or group work inspired students to take the initiative or to volunteer for complex writing assignments and additional projects; they were more willing to do so while working in groups than when given an individual assignment. In addition, peer-paired teaching or group work encouraged social integration, which can motivate students to move toward self-directness. Valez et al. (2011) reported that the Millennial generation's learning increased when working in groups.

How to Identify Student Leaders in the Classroom?

Two weeks into the semester, the instructor's goal is to find leaders in the class. They are planted around the room; they just need to be found. Leaders are more talkative; they are often seen explaining something a teacher has said to those around them or to someone sitting on the other side of the classroom who just asked a question among peers but not openly to the teacher. After the writing teacher has identified leaders in the classroom, it is possible to determine how many groups to form. Keep all information confidential until after the pre-writing assessments have been graded. Then purposefully form groups based on students' writing strengths and weaknesses (Elbow, 1998), placing two or three, but not more than four, students in a group.

Peer-paired teaching lends itself to an environment in which students work in groups during instructional writing activities (Napier & Gershenfeld, 2004; Valez et al., 2011). Peer-paired teaching or group work is useful for peer reviewing, assigned chapter readings, or group discussions. By placing student leaders in each group, the class can benefit from peer-paired teaching and group work, which may help a struggling writer reduce writing errors or overcome bad habits (Elbow, 1998). Two or three good writers can help proofread assignments. In addition, peer-paired teaching and group work can free the teacher to initiate instructional classroom coaching.

How to Shift towards an Instructional Writing Coaching?

Johns Hopkins University outlined concepts on instructional educational coaching (Lacefield, 2014). Instructional educational coaching is a framework for effective mediation in the classroom. It focuses on self-directed learning at the guidance of the teacher (Perna, 2013). In this context, the term "instructional writing coaching" will be used. This is a powerful tool for stimulating a positive writing environment. It can help undergird insecure writers in a diverse learning environment (Carter, 2007; Costa & Garmston, 1985; Holly, 2014).

Moreover, Costa and Robert (2002) reported that under the auspices of instructional educational coaching, teachers become less prescriptive in their attitudes toward students, and students become more in charge of their learning and their lives. This technique is an excellent way for writing teachers to work closely with students affected by negative predispositions. Using the coaching approach will permit writing teachers to shift from the role of teacher to that of facilitator. Eventually, instructional writing coaching can encourage stronger teacher–student relationships (Costa & Robert, 2002). Remember, though, that before instructional writing coaching can work effectively in a diverse learning environment, students affected with negative predispositions need to feel a connection to the environment; they must feel safe and included (Cartwright, 1955; Costa & Garmston, 1985; Holly, 2014). Thus, a positive learning environment must be established before these greater changes to technique can be successfully implemented.

Five Keys: Becoming an Effective Writing Coach

Five keys can help you develop as an effective instructional writing coach in the classroom:

1. Listen: Listen first to understand, then listen to be understood. Professional writing teachers must

actively listen to their students to build trusting relations.

2. Be positive: Positive language can encourage a student to at least try. It is critical for professional writing teachers to understand and implement positive language aspects such as pitch, tone, and volume when communicating with this sensitive group.

3. Be caring: Professional writing teachers should display a caring attitude, one signaling genuineness and honesty.

4. Practice self-development: Professional writing instructors should continue to perfect their teaching methodologies and philosophical views by staying abreast of new theories, strategies, and research topics on developing and improving written communication skills at college.

5. Be a guide: Teachers should help students to set realistic learning goals and then follow up by counseling those students on their progress so they will know exactly what is expected of them in the course.

Finally, to be an effective writing coach, a professional writing teacher want to provide specific but positive feedback—not just to your students who are affected by negative predispositions, but to all students. The goal is to give feedback on how well or poorly your students performed on assignments, but such feedback must be given by positive affirmation. The positive feedback can be corrective, but it must be given verbally or in writing. Effective coaching can offer students a flexible solution for fulfilling their writing goals.

How to Avoid an Authoritarian Teaching Practice?

Writing teachers should avoid an authoritarian teaching practice. According to Holt, Freire, and Illich (2013), an *authoritarian* teaching practice is one in which writing teachers impose their will by sheer force or by using their institutional power. An example of an authoritarian writing teacher is one who expels from their class students who have stopped participating or who grades their assignments differently.

Brookfield (2006) advised teachers to maintain a professional attitude in the classroom at all times. As writing teachers, we will surely encounter and teach students affected by negative predispositions. In such situations, a teacher can become intensely frustrated, particularly while teaching new concepts, similar to Malamud at Oregon State University (Chantrill, 2008). Several writing teachers have reported experiencing undue stress trying to teach certain students (Chantrill, 2008;

Holt, et al., 2013). Knowing that stress is bound to occur at some point, if a writing teacher feels overwhelmed or frustrated, he or she must take a deep breath and repeat the positive quote, statement, or philosophy that was chosen at the beginning of the semester. This statement isn't just for the students; it's for us as well.

Summary

This guide is a helpful tool for teachers. It exposes educational perspectives on how negative predispositions prevents a student from performing at high levels. Negative predispositions known as psychological barriers derived from years of red ink marks put on graded writing assignments by writing teachers over time (Lindemann and Anderson, 2001). The easy read suggests strategies and classroom management practices useful for lessening the effects of students' negative predispositions. It is a helpful guide to aid writing teachers.

Joining Forces to Combat Bad Writing

We must join our forces to help our students write with confidence. We must continue to explore topics on students' cultural backgrounds and there affects. We must begin building upon the positive to lessen the effects of negative predispositions. We must plan, prepare, and position ourseves to create effective and meaningful classrooms to stir a spirit of inquiry and motivate our students toward a pleasant journey for learning to write in college. We must keep students from walking out on the valuable opportunities education can afford them. We must continue encouraging college administrators to allocate funds for creating innovation programs for more one-on-one support. We must do all we can to make our world of education better as we embark upon a new Millennium.

Finally, in similar words of Howe and Strauss (2007) that institutions that ride out the trends of the Millennial era might risk damaging their reputations by lowering their standards to conform to this generation's preferences. If institutions take this risk, it may take them years to rebuild their good reputation; however, if institutions do not take on this challenge to meet the Millennials' needs, they would be doing a disservice to a generation that they had dedicated themselves to serving. In other words, colleges and adult education programs that plan appropriately have an extraordinary opportunity to stay competitive.

REFERENCES

Bland, H. W., Melton, B. F., Wells, P. S. B., & Bigham, L. (2012). Stress tolerance: New challenges for millennial college students. *College Student Journal, 32,* 362–375. Retrieved from http://digitalcommons. georgiasouthern.edu/commhealth-facpubs/32.

Brookfield, S. D. (2006). *The skillful teacher: On techniques, trust, and responsiveness in the classroom* (2nd ed.). San Francisco, CA: John Wiley & Sons, Inc.

Burke, K., L. (2002). *An inquiry into the Schoolwide enrichment model at Mercer Middle School.* (Doctoral dissertation). College of Graduate Studies of Georgia Southern University, Statesboro, GA.

Caffarella, R. S. (2007). *Planning programs for adult learners.* San Francisco, CA: Jossey-Bass, Inc.

California Council for Adult Education (CCAE). (2014). *CCAE: A complete history.* Retrieved from www. ccaestate.org/ccae-a-complete-history/.

Carlson, R. A. (1970). Americanization as an early twentieth-century adult education movement. *The History of Education, 10*(4), 440–464.

Carter, T. (2007). Reaching your millennials: A fresh look at freshman orientation. *Tennessee Libraries, 57*(2), 1–4.

Cartwright, M. A. (1955). *Ten years of adult education.* New York, NY: MacMillan.

Chantrill, C. (2008). The U.S. can't pass English 101. *American Thinker.* Retrieved from http://www.americanthinker. com/2008/05/us_can't_pass_english_101. html#ixzz3mTaivvDq.

Complete College America. (2014). Reports. Retrieved from http://www.completecollege.org.

Conklin, T. A. (2012). Making it personal: The importance of student experience, in Creating autonomy-supportive classrooms for millennial learners. The Journal of Management Education, 37 (4), 499- 538. Retrieved from http://www.sagepub.com/journalsP ermissions. nav. doi: 10.1177/1052562912456296. *Resource Development International Research Conference.* Austin, TX. Retrieved from http://www.lindenwood.edu/education/andragogy/andragogy/2011/ Cooper_Henschke_2003_2004.pdf.

Cornell, R. (2013). Paradigm for the new millennium: How professors will certainly change. (Essay summation, University of Central Florida). Retrieved from http:// *files.eric.ed.gov/fulltext/ ED484992.pdf.*

Costa, A., & Robert, G. (2002). Cognitive coaching: A foundation for Renaissance schools (2nd ed.). Norwood, MA: Christopher-Gordon.

Darkenwald, G. G., & Merriam, S. B. (1982). *Adult education: Foundation of practice.* New York: Harper and Row. *Dictionary of Human Resources and Personnel Management.* (2006). "Andragogy." Retrieved from http://www.credorereference.com.

Dobrin, S. I. (2015). *Writing situations.* Boston, MA: Pearson Education, Inc.

Elbow, P. (1998). *Writing with Power: Techniques for Mastering the Writing Process* (2nd ed.). New York, NY: Oxford University Press.

Elias, J. C., & Merriam, S. B. (1995). *The philosophical foundation of adult education.* Malabar, FL: Krieger.

Falk, C. F., & Blaylock, B. K. (2010). Strategically planning campuses for the "newer students" in higher education. *Academy of Educational Leadership Journal, 14*(3), 15–38.

Freire, P., & Macedo, (2005). *Literacy and critical Pedagogy.* Reader Continuum International Publishing Group: New York New York.

Gabriel, D. D. (2014, December 2). Why so many students are spending six years getting a college degree. *Washington Post.* Retrieved from https://www.washingtonpost.com/news/wonk/wp/2014/12/02/why-so-many-students-are-spending-six-years-getting-a-college-deg.

Green, R. (2000). *Natural forces: How to Significantly increase student achievement in the third millennium.* Monticello, FL: Education Services Consortium, Inc. /pdf. http://search.proquest.com/docview/1328996148?accountid=14800.

Haley, M. H., & Alsweel, R. A. (2012). Bridging instructional gaps in preparing to teach millennial language learners. Theory and Practice in Language Studies, 2 (5), 865-876. Available from http://search.proquest.com/docview/1328996148?accountid=14800.

Heitin, L. (2016, February). Will the Common Core step up schools' focus on grammar? *Education Week*, 35(22). Retrieved from http://www.edweek.org/ew/articles/2016/02/24/willthecommoncorestep-upschools.html? tkn=PURFB6b7ntI9gh3XSR-jKA%2Fuf%2BGTguzSFBdxI&print=1.

Hendricks, L. (2017). A Narrative Study: Investigating the Meaning of Negative Predispositions towards Writing. (Doctoral dissertation). Valdosta State University, Valdosta, Georgia. Available from DSpace thesis database: http://hdl.handle.net/10428/2835.

Hershey, P., Blanchard, K., & Johnson, D. (1996). *Management of organizational behavior: Utilizing human resources.* Upper Saddle River, NJ: Prentice Hall.

Holt, J. C, Freire, P., & Illich, I. (2013). *Un-schooling and free schools.* Retrieved from http://www.fifthestate.org/archive/388-winter- 2013/unschooling-and-free-schools.

Holly, M. E. (2014). *Experiential learning and student engagement: Meaningful learner outcomes as articulated.* (Doctoral dissertation). Retrieved from ProQuest database. (UMI No. 3628187).

Howe, N., & Strauss, W. (2007). *Millennials go to college: Strategies for a new generation on campus, recruiting and admissions, campus life, and the classroom (*2nd ed.). Great Falls, VA: Life Course Associates.

Knowles, M. S. (1980b). *The modern practice of adult education: From pedagogy to andragogy* (Rev. ed). New York, NY: Association Press.

Knowles, M. S. (1989). *The making of an*

adult educator: An autobiography. San Francisco, CA: Jossey-Bass.

Knowles, M. S., Holton, E. F., & Swanson, R. A. (2012). *The adult learner: The definitive classic in adult education and human development.* London and New York: Routledge.

Lacefield, R. (2014). *Adult education in practice: Teaching methods and courses.* Retrieved from http://roberta.tripod.com/adulted/methods.htm.

Lindeman, E. C. (1925; 1961). *The meaning of adult education.* New York, NY: New Republic. (Republished in 1961 by Harvest House).

Lindemann, E., & Anderson, D. (2001). *A rhetoric for writing teachers* (4th ed.). New York, Oxford: Oxford University Press.

Levine, H. G., & Kirst, M. W. (2015, April). Why colleges should care about the Common Core. *Education Week Commentary, 34(*27).

Mackeracher, D. (2004). *Making sense of adult learning* (2nd ed.). Toronto: University of Toronto Press.

McLaughlin, M. (2010). *Content area reading: Teaching and learning in an age of multiple literacies.* Boston, MA: Pearson Education, Inc.

Merriam, S. B., Caffarella, R. S., & Baumgartner, L. M. (2006*). Learning in adulthood: A comprehensive guide* (3rd ed.). San Francisco, CA: Jossey-Bass.

Merriam, S. B, & Brockett, R. G. (2007). *The profession and practice of adult education: An introduction.* San Francisco, CA: John Wiley & Sons, Inc.

Merriam, S. B, & Bierema, L. L. (2014). *Adult learning: Linking theory and practice.*San Francisco, CA: John Wiley & Sons, Inc.

National Assessment of Adult Literacy. (2015). Report on National Education Association.

Napier, R. W., & Gershenfeld, M. K. (2004). *Groups: Theory and practice.* Boston, MA: Houghton Mifflin.

Ormond, J. E. (2009). *Essentials of educational psychology* (2nd ed.). Saddle River, NJ: Pearson Education, Inc.

Perna, M. C. (2013). Tools for schools. Handout. Retrieved from http://www.tfsresults.com/contact-us/.

Savannah Technical College Fundamentals of English: ENGL1010. The English 1010 textbook. Boston, MA: Pearson Education, Inc.

Schon, D. (1987). Educating the reflective practitioner: Toward a new design for teaching and learning in the professions. San Francisco, CA: Jossey-Bass.

Scriven, M. & Paul, R. (1996). Defining critical thinking: A draft statement for the National Council for Excellence in Critical Thinking. Retrieved from http://www.criticalthinking.org/University/university/library.nclk. from ProQuest Dissertations and Thesis Database. (UMI No. 3437607).

Surowiecki, J. (2005). *The wisdom of crowds.* New York, NY, and Toronto, Canada: Random House, Inc.

Technical College Systems of Georgia System Office Data Warehouse. (2015). Learning support student overview. Retrieved from https:/ https://gosa. georgia.gov/complete-college-georgia-overview.

Technical College System of Georgia (TCSG). (2015). English 1010–Fundamentals Of English I Standard (version 201003L). Retrieved from https: //kms.tcsg.edu/CDbUser/crs/CrsDisplay. aspx?crsid=503.

Tough, A. (1967). *Learning without a teacher.* (Education Research Series No. 3.) Toronto: Ontario Institute for Studies in Education.

Tough, A. (2006). International Adult and Continuing Education Hall of Fame. Norman, OK: The University of Oklahoma. Retrieved from http:// www.halloffame.outreach.ou.edu/2006/tough. html.

Turner, P., & Thompson, E. (2014). College retention initiatives are meeting the needs of millennial freshman students. *College Student Journal, 48*(1), 94–103. Retrieved from https://www.ques-tia.com/library/journal/1G1-372252070/col-lege-retention-initiatives-meeting-the-needs-of college-students.

U. S. Department of Education National Center for Education Statistics. (NCES). (2015). *Digest of Education Statistics, 2013.* (NCES 2015-011).

Valez, J. J, Cano, J., Whittington, M. S., & Wolf, K. J. (2011). Cultivating changes through peer teaching. *Journal of Agricultural Education, 52*(1), 40–49.

West, L. I. (2005). Adult education's contributions to society evolves as our needs change. *California Department of Education.* Retrieved from http://www.questia.com/read/adult-education.

ABOUT THE AUTHOR

LaRonce M. Hendricks is an effective teacher, leader, and public speaker. She earned a doctorate of Education degree in Leadership from Valdosta State University and a master of Education degree in Adult Education from Armstrong State University. Her passion for education became apparent when she taught English courses at Savannah Technical College, which sparked her interest in her dissertation research, which explored how to get technical college students who are beginning their course work to become comfortable and skilled at the writing requirements required by higher education. In addition, her ability in relating to adults as an instructor has been apparent in her work on Fort. Stewart Army base working with veterans to help them adjust back to civilian life. She has contributed to the scholarship and integrity of the field of adult and career education, and she has proven that perseverance yields great dividends if one works hard enough at an endeavor.

What's Coming Next?

"There is no royal path to good writing, and such paths as exist . . . lead through the jungles of the self, the world, and the craft"—Jessamyn West (1957).

According to West, a path to good writing largely arises from "...the jungles of the self, the world, and the craft," (p. 1) and, as such, one must begin the quest to understand this journey through examining his or her own jungles.

In this writing, the author explores the journey of writing through the lens of first-year technical college students between the ages of 18 and 24. An interpretation of the subject of writing based on the study: A Narrative Phenomenological Study: An Investigation into the Meaning of Negative Predipositions. The world of grammar and the craft of writing are investigated to find a royal path to good writing.

A self-reflection is taken for an autobiographical connection to expose negative predispositions toward writing in college.

Chantrill (2008) and Gabriel (2014) argued that some freshman students panicked when they were told that they must take a first-year English course. That some students would emotionally detach themselves from courses or stop participating altogether when pursuing difficult writing assignments, such as a college research paper (Elias, 1995; Holly, 2015).

The narrative builds on theoretical foundations of constructivist perspectives, andragogy, and educational psychology. It presents relevant information to support how negative predispositions can affect a first-year college student's ability to improve and develop communication skills using written methods in academic programs (Hendricks, 2017).